T0004794

SHARK ATTACK
Stories of Survival

Robyn P. Watts

KNOWLEDGE BOOKS

Teacher Notes:

Learn more about one of the world's oldest and most dangerous predators, the shark. Explore the differences between sharks and dolphins, discover how deadly some sharks can be to humans and learn about the important role they play in the underwater food chain. Environmental conservation and the impact on tourism at our beaches are possible avenues to explore further.

Discussion points for consideration:

1. Recent shark attacks on swimming beaches have reignited discussions about shark culling. Discuss the pros and cons of this option.

2. Discuss the ways you can minimize being attacked by a shark when swimming. What would you do if you were in danger of being attacked?

3. Explore various things that people are inventing to deter sharks from attacking them.

Sight words, difficult to decode words, and infrequent words to be introduced and practiced before reading this book:

dolphins, difference, vertical, horizontal, motion, holidaying, identified, puncture, thrashing, airlifted, hospital, recovery, nostril, detected, amazing, armor, continually, algae, disappearing, cartilage, interview, temperate, wobbegong, snorkelling, Queensland, championship, ancient, dangerous, accidentally.

Contents

1. Are All Sharks Dangerous?

2. Shark Attack on a Reef

3. About Sharks

4. How Many Teeth do Sharks Have?

5. Are Sharks Important?

6. Sharks in the Food Chain

7. The Great White Pointer Sharks

8. Other Dangerous Sharks

1. Are All Sharks Dangerous?

Would you go swimming if you knew what was in the water around you?

On a warm summer day, the surf looks inviting. It is a good time to get cool and catch some waves.

Everyone enjoys a day at the beach. What do you like to do when you go to the beach?

Most people enjoy swimming in the ocean. It is very important to swim where there is a beach patrol.

What is the difference between sharks and dolphins? How do surfers tell the difference between sharks and dolphins?

Sometimes dolphins can be seen swimming in the waves. When you see a dolphin they are usually in a group called a pod. Dolphins breathe air so they come to the surface and dive again.

A dolphin's tail is horizontal, and they use them in an up-and-down motion to swim. A shark's tail fins are vertical, and they use the fins in a side-to-side motion to swim.

2. Shark Attack on a Reef

In January 2019, a family was holidaying at North West Island off Queensland, Australia. The family had travelled to the island.

They were hoping to see baby turtles. The mother turtle lays the eggs in the sand. The baby turtles hatch out and crawl towards the ocean. The family were hoping to see baby turtles crawling on the sand.

On the island, the tides change every day. During low tide, the water flows off the reef. At low tide, you can walk on the coral and see little coral rock pools. At high tide, the water rushes over the coral. The fish come in with the rush of the water. The water comes in very fast and floods the coral. The sea covers the coral. The high tide is when the fish come in to eat. The big fish eat other fish hiding in the corals.

This is what happened the day Miah, a seven-year-old, got bitten by a shark.

The water was at the high tide mark. The coral was covered with water. There were lots of fish coming into the reef with the water flowing in. The shark came in chasing fish.

Miah did not see the shark as she was just at the edge of the water. She was paddling knee-deep in the water. She did not see the shark swimming closer.

The shark came swimming close to the water's edge and spotted Miah's leg.

The shark bit Miah's leg. Miah's father saw the shark. He ran into the water and tried to get Miah away from the shark.

Miah's dad kicked the shark's head. The shark did not let Miah's leg go. Miah's father kicked the shark's head again and again.

At last, the shark let Miah's leg go.

Miah's father grabbed her in his arms and ran up the beach.

There was a lot of blood in the water. The shark was identified as a lemon shark.

Miah's leg has twenty shark teeth puncture marks. Miah is lucky that she still has her leg.

Sharks have a lot of teeth. These teeth are for tearing and slicing. Sharks have multiple rows of teeth. If you are bitten by a shark they will leave a lot of holes in your skin.

 Scan the link to see what the shark looks like swimming in the ocean.

The people of North West Island believe that the same lemon shark had attacked another person a few weeks earlier.

Miah's father, David, said "I heard her screaming, I could see the shark's tail thrashing in the water and knew it was biting her."

Miah was airlifted to hospital with long cuts to her leg, and 20 wounds in her foot. Miah has made a full recovery.

The authorities have asked all fishermen not to leave any trace of fish scraps in the ocean around the island. Some people saw fish scraps in the water where Miah was bitten. Fish scraps had been left a day earlier.

3. About Sharks

Sharks can smell. They can smell fish and blood. They can smell even just a small trace of blood from many miles away.

How do sharks smell blood under water?

Sharks smell through the seawater. Humans smell and breathe through their nose. Sharks only smell through their nose. Sharks do not breathe through their nose. Where is the nose on a shark?

A shark's nostrils are on the underside of the snout. Sharks can smell food miles away. Any flesh fluid released into the ocean is likely to be detected by sharks.

Some sharks can find fish by their movement and heartbeat. They must have amazing senses to be able to pick up tiny heartbeats many miles away!

Do sharks sleep? Sharks do not sleep like humans. They have rest times and active times. Some sharks do not sleep at all. The nurse shark has holes where they force water over their gills. The nurse shark rests when this is happening but still needs to move.

What does sharkskin feel like?

Sharkskin feels like sandpaper. It is a tough armor and can injure prey such as smaller fish.

4. How Many Teeth do Sharks Have?

Most sharks have fifteen rows of teeth. They have teeth in the upper jaw and the lower jaw.

They have a series of teeth behind the active first row. Sharks lose their teeth often.

Sharks have powerful jaws. Their jaws are the most powerful of all animals. They can easily crush the bones of large fish and seals.

Sharks can sometimes have up to 50,000 teeth in a lifetime. Sharks continually lose and replace their teeth over their life.

Where in the world do most shark attacks occur? Australia has had some attacks recently. However, most shark attacks occur off the coast of Florida in the USA.

Sharks move over a large area. Some sharks travel between countries. Other sharks stay close to a reef their entire life.

5. Are Sharks Important?

What happens if we kill all the sharks in the oceans? If we kill all sharks, then we will not get bitten or eaten. But the oceans will start to get very sick. Sharks have a very important job. Sharks are the garbage trucks of the ocean.

On a coral reef the sharks swim around looking for food. If they feel, smell, or hear a dying fish or animal, they will rush in. When you hook a fish, it struggles to get free. At that moment, the sharks from all over the reef know there is a fish struggling. They race in to eat the fish. If you are not fast to bring in your catch you will be left with just the head. The shark quickly eats the fish. Sharks can also eat dead whales.

Most of the hundreds of sharks are harmless. Sharks are very important to keep the oceans clean of dead and sick animals.

Sharks are part of the web of living things in the ocean. The oceans have many different animals, and each has a certain section where they fit. Some fish eat crabs and smaller fish, and become food for larger fish. If there are no large fish eating these smaller fish, then the numbers of these fish grow. Soon there are too many of this type of fish and they eat all the smaller fish and crabs.

6. Sharks in the Food Chain

What happens when we take sharks out of the web of living things? Let us look at a food chain in the ocean.

Seaweed and algae – this is the first level in the chain. These grow all over rocks and on the floor of the sea.

Plant eaters – some of the fish, crabs and shellfish eat the algae and seaweed. These fish also eat the coral.

Fish eaters – larger fish eat the plant-eating fish. These fish are built to hunt fish.

Large fish – the big fish swim very fast and can eat any of these fish. The big, fast fish eat only fish, not seaweed.

If you kill all the sharks, then nothing eats the bigger fish. The oceans start to become sick as the reef is no longer in balance. Changing the balance can cause too many small fish to be eaten, which can cause too much coral algae to grow. The reef is out of balance, and one plant or animal takes control until it runs out of food and then dies.

Sharks play an important part in keeping the ocean healthy. They are not easily replaced by dolphins or turtles. If there are too many sharks they will eat all the dead and injured fish, until there is not enough food. Then the numbers will drop back down and find a balance. This image shows a tiger shark eating a dead whale.

Sharks are taken for their fins. The body of the shark is thrown away. The only part that is kept is the fin. This is a terrible waste of food. It also means that many sharks are killed and there are places without sharks. This means that the ocean is no longer in balance.

Taking just the fins of sharks will reduce the shark numbers and cause problems. The sharks need to be protected from this waste of food. We need to look after shark numbers to stop them from disappearing completely.

7. The Great White Shark

However, there are some sharks which are very dangerous.

Great white sharks have eaten legs and whole people. In 1908, a man fell from a jetty at Thursday Island in Queensland, and was totally eaten.

In 2014, a lady was eaten whole whilst swimming at Tathra Beach in NSW.

A surfer lost his legs completely at Shelley Beach, Ballina in 2015.

Do sharks eat dolphins? Some sharks such as the great white shark eat dolphins and seals. Tiger sharks and bull sharks also eat dolphins.

Dolphins look after each other. When a shark attacks dolphins, the pod will work together and fight off the shark.

Sharks and dolphins eat the same fish and can be found in the same areas.

Dolphins hunt in pods and work as a team to get fish into a small area. Sharks hunt alone and feed off whatever they can find.

Dolphins are mammals and have a large brain. They are smart and have many ways of catching fish.

Sharks are a very old form of sea life. Sharks have cartilage instead of bones. Sharks were on the Earth before the dinosaurs.

In the "Jaws" movie, the famous shark was the white pointer. The white pointer has no other animal to eat it. Though sometimes the killer whale has been known to eat a white pointer. The white shark can grow up to 20 feet in length.

The white sharks can live to the age of seventy. They can swim at a speed of 35 miles per hour.

A man was mauled while scuba diving in 2020. He was diving off an island near the town of Esperance, in Western Australia. He survived to tell the tale.

The Aussie world surfing champion Mick Fanning was attacked by a great white shark. The whole attack was caught on film because it happened at the world surfing championships in South Africa at Jeffries Bay, near Port Elizabeth.

This is at the southern end of South Africa and is the home of the great white sharks. The great white pointer sharks chase after whales and seals.

Scan this QR code to watch Mick Fanning's account of his ordeal.

In this film Mick explains how he managed to escape the great white pointer shark. What a shock for the surfing championship organisers to find a great white pointer shark close to the event! The water was foaming and hard to see below.

What would you do if it happened to you?

Mick Fanning explains in the interview that he was in a state of shock. Who would expect a white pointer shark to be that close in the water? After the shark attack, Mick overcame his fears and his nightmares, and started to think of surfing again. Soon after he went surfing on his board again.

He was so close that he saw the white
face of the white pointer.

8. Other Dangerous Sharks

Another shark that attacks humans is the tiger shark. It lives in tropical and temperate waters. The tiger shark travels over shallow reefs, in harbours and canals. They live mostly in the Pacific Ocean. They can see well in the low light underwater, and grow to a length of about 18 feet. On the side of their bodies a tiger pattern can be seen.

The three main sharks that eat humans are the white shark, the tiger shark and the bull shark.

Bull sharks eats humans if they get a chance.

Bull sharks are unusual because they can live both in seawater and freshwater. They live in rivers and lakes. In 2018, a bull shark swam up the main street in Ingham in Queensland during a flood. No one was attacked at the time. Bull sharks swim in shallow water.

The bull shark can be found on the Gold Coast in rivers, lakes and canals. There are also bull sharks in the Brisbane River and Moreton Bay. Care must be taken in these waters.

Are there any sharks that do not bite humans?

It is not the type of animal you want to be friendly with. There is a bottom feeder shark called the wobbegong shark. It hides itself in seaweed underwater. Some say they aren't dangerous to swim near. They're generally harmless to humans, unless they're stirred. Touching or cornering a wobbegong, or accidentally stepping on one, could cause it to bite! It gives you a shock when you are snorkelling underwater and you feel a pair of eyes watching you. Looking around, you spot the eyes. It is a wobbegong!

You move very carefully and fast, away from the shark. Don't take risks with any sharks.

Word Bank

wobbegong	survived
snorkelling	ancient
occurred	mammals
unusual	advanced
Queensland	dangerous
Esperance	important
processes	accidentally
carefully	
championship	